AF484835

# Hypothyroidism Healed

## Combined Holistic Approach:
## Yoga, Reiki, Mantra & Crystals

**Jyotsnaa G Bansal**

PAPER TOWNS
PUBLISHERS

First published by
Papertowns Publishers
72, Vishwanath Dham Colony,
Niwaru Road, Jhotwara,
Jaipur, 302012

Hypothyroidism Healed Combined Holistic Approach: Yoga, Reiki, Mantra & Crystals



ISBN Print Book – 978-93-6185-514-6



Printed in India

Cover Credits: Jyotsnaa G Bansal

# Praise for Hypothyroidism Healed

"*Hypothyroidism Healed* showcases the amazing journey of the author to rise above the limitations the disease imposes. It gives great insight into the practical applicability of adopting a holistic approach to a debilitating lifestyle syndrome. With her grit and determination Jyotsnaa moulded various modalities honing them to work in her favour! I am sure many in the same condition will find it to be an inspiring manual to put them back on the path of good health!" - **Meenu Minocha,** *Author, Reiki Grandmaster and Holistic Practitioner*

*(Reiki Grandmaster Meenu Minocha has been working with Holistic Energies for almost fifteen years and has mentored innumerable students, myself being one of them.)*

*"**Hypothyroidism Healed** - Jyotsnaa's journey to healing through Yoga is a masterpiece in itself. Her strength and resilience inspire me. It shows that with the right steps and right approach, anyone can get past these health challenges. It's not just about taking medicine, but also about making smart choices every day about your health, how you live, eating better and keeping active. So inspiring!*

I think anyone dealing with similar health stuff, or anyone who knows someone who is, should give this book a read. It's written in plain language just like a conversation with a good friend —straightforward and encouraging. You don't feel like you're getting lost in medical talk at all, which makes it super easy to understand and relate to. I wish her best of luck to keep painting her path with grace and courage". = **Anjana Singh**, *Kathak Exponent, Former Cultural Attaché ( Kathak Dance Teacher ) at SVCC,* **Embassy of India , Suriname, South America**

*Anjana Singh, M. A.(Eng.), holds a*

- *PG Diploma from Kathak Kendra [The National Institute of Kathak Dance], New Delhi,*
- *Kathak Praveen from Prayag Sangeet Samiti, Allahabad and*
- *Sangeet Prabhakar in Vocals.*

*(She has performed extensively in India and abroad in places like Singapore, Pakistan, Indonesia and Australia etc. She has worked with some eminent personalities in the dance world which includes Ms. Sarmishtha Mukherjee, daughter of the former Hon'ble President of India.*

*In August 2021 Anjana was recruited by Indian Council for Cultural Relations(ICCR) as the Kathak Dance Teacher at the Swami Vivekananda Cultural Centre [SVCC], Embassy of India, Paramaribo, Suriname, South America. Looking at her good work her tenure was extended by another year till 2023 by the Council).*

"**Hypothyroidism Healed** details how Jyotsnaa managed to overcome thyroid issues by sticking to Yoga routine and Alternative Holistic Healing modalities. It's a real game-changer as finding strength and balance through Yoga is truly inspiring. For anyone looking for a natural way to improve their thyroid health and overall well-being, this book makes you believe that with the right approach, anyone can overcome their health hurdles. Definitely a must-read if you're on a similar path."- **Dr. Somveer Arya,** *Director of Indian Culture - Swami Vivekananda Cultural Centre,* ***Embassy of India, Suriname, South America***

*(Dr. Somveer Arya, Ph.D.(Yoga), Yoga Acharya, has been actively associated with the field of Yoga for fifteen (15) years and has been doing research work in Yoga with an inquisitive spirit for the last twelve (12) years.*

*Dr. Somveer Arya has also served for two years as an Indian Culture and Yoga teacher in the Indian Consulate in Atlanta, USA under the Ministry of External Affairs, Government of India. He has worked as Lead Examiner as well as Yoga Head in YCB of Ministry of AYUSH. Before this, Dr. Arya has worked as the first Yoga expert of UGC for two consecutive years. Till now hundreds of national and international yoga workshops have been successfully organized by them.*

*Dr. Arya is a Yoga Practitioner, Spokesperson and Writer. Till now, six of his books have been published.)*

*"**Hypothyroidism Healed** details Jyotsnaa's personal journey of overcoming thyroid issues. With her husband Navit's support, she turned to Alternative Healing methods coupled with Homeopathic medicines and lifestyle changes, which collectively aided her recovery. It includes the Yoga poses specifically beneficial for thyroid health and the use of Mantras for spiritual and physical wellness.*

An interesting addition is the mnemonic for learning the zodiac signs, which could benefit beginners in Astrology and Numerology. This book has unique contents of self-realisation about the disease, impact and solutions based on day-to-day observations of the individual health and well-being and the same can be helpful for everyone who care about their health."- **Prof. (Dr.) Ajay Kumar Bhatt,** *Director, Amity Law School,* **Amity University, Gurugram, Haryana**

*(Prof. Dr Ajay Kumar Bhatt, D.Phil, NET, LLM, LLB, has vast experience of teaching for almost 2 decades at various esteemed law colleges. Dr. Bhatt is an expert in Jurisprudence and Constitutional laws. There are several research papers to his credit published in renowned law journals and magazines. He has authored the book titled – Essays on Contemporary Legal Issues. He has been a guide to more than 12 research scholars.)*

"Jyotsnaa's journey from diagnosis to healing is not just a personal triumph, but a roadmap for those seeking alternative paths to wellness." - In **"Hypothyroidism Healed,"** Jyotsnaa shares her inspiring story of overcoming thyroid dysfunction through a unique blend of Yoga, Reiki, Mantras and Crystals. Is Hypothyroidism affecting your well-being? Are you seeking a path to greater vitality and resilience? Discover the profound impact of holistic practices and embark on your own path to healing and transformation"- **Kulwinder Singh,** *IT Director – Cybersecurity,* **Siemens USA**

*(Kulwinder Singh is a senior IT leader with over 20 years of global IT infrastructure and people leadership experience in large organizations. He serves on the advisory boards of several startups. He is an alumnus of IIT Delhi and Delhi College of Engineering.)*

*"Hypothyroidism Healed* narrates Jyotsnaa's journey from diagnosis to victory over thyroid dysfunction. Faced with the prospect of lifelong medication, Jyotsnaa and her husband, **Adv. Navit Bansal,** embrace holistic healing modalities.

Through Yoga, Reiki, Mantras and Crystals, Jyotsnaa discovers a path to wellness that transcends conventional medicine. Her story, woven with personal anecdotes and practical insights, offers hope and empowerment to those grappling with similar challenges.

This book is not just a guide; it's a heartfelt narrative that resonates with readers on a deep level. Jyotsnaa's candid sharing of her struggles and victories creates a profound connection, inspiring others to explore alternative avenues to health and vitality." **Sumeet Dhall,** *Head - Finance & Accounts, SEEDS Fincap P. Ltd. (NBFC)*

*(**Sumeet Dhall** is a qualified CA, with more than 20 years long experience of entrepreneurial and Financial Management Skills, heading the Accounts and Finance department of Seeds Fincap Pvt Ltd (NBFC). Prior to that, he worked with Satya MicroCapital Limited, a NBFC-MFI since its inception for 4 Years as Head-Accounts.)*

"Jyotsnaa bears a spiritual, creative and a holistic demeanour. Her creative approach to health resolutions resonates with a respect for mother nature. This effort of sharing valuable self-learnt lessons through her book *"Hypothyroidism Healed"*, while holistically resolving her own issues will surely benefit many. May the Divine bless her with great success in this noble service to mankind."- **Sqn Ldr (Retd) Ashutosh Bahuguna,** *Reiki Grandmaster & Founder – BetterAll*

*(**Sqn Ldr (Retd) Ashutosh Bahuguna** is an alumnus of the National Defence Academy who served in the Indian Air Force and United Nations for 13 years as an officer flying helicopters. After graduating from Management Development Institute, Gurgaon he ventured into the corporate in India and Dubai, UAE for a few years. Since 2013, he has been practicing and teaching Reiki Healing, Crystal Healing and Dowsing having learnt the same from Reiki Healing Foundation. Past Life Hypnotherapy, Emotional Freedom Technique, subconscious management, healing by Vedic Mantras and Santana Dharma devotional methods are also a part of his practice.)*

# Discover Holistic Healing

As someone who has Hypothyroidism, I can relate to the stress, fatigue, anxiety, weight gain and lifelong dependence on medicines. Jyotsnaa's journey in overcoming hypothyroidism through alternative and holistic healing, penned in the form of this book, is a blessing for all those going through the same emotional upheaval.

**Dr. Monica Yadav**

*Professor, IILM Law School,*

*IILM University, Gurugram*

In the pursuit of holistic wellness, we are often drawn to explore the profound intersections between ancient wisdom and modern science. **"Hypothyroidism Healed: Combined Holistic Approach Yoga, Reiki, Mantra & Crystals"** is a beacon of light in this journey, offering a comprehensive roadmap to healing that integrates the timeless practices of Yoga, Reiki, Mantra and Crystals.

In today's fast-paced world, where stress and anxiety seem to be constant companions, it's all too easy for our bodies to fall out of balance. One of the most common imbalances affecting millions worldwide is hypothyroidism. This condition not only impacts physical health but also affects mental and emotional well-being.

Within the pages of this book, readers will discover a sanctuary of healing wisdom that transcends conventional approaches. Through the synergistic combination of Yoga's mindful movement, Reiki's energy healing, Mantra's vibrational resonance and Crystals' innate power, individuals are invited to embark on a transformative journey towards holistic well-being.

What sets this book apart is its unwavering commitment of the Author to addressing the root causes of hypothyroidism while honouring the interconnectedness of Mind, Body and Spirit. By embracing this multifaceted approach, readers can unlock the body's innate ability to heal and restore balance, not only to the thyroid gland but to the entire being.

As you immerse yourself in the wisdom contained within these pages, may you find solace, empowerment and the tools you need to embark on your own healing odyssey. Let this book be your trusted guide as you reclaim your vitality, reconnect with your inner wisdom and awaken to the radiant potential of your true self.

With deepest gratitude for the author's dedication to healing and transformation.

**Prof. (Dr) Monica Yadav**

*Prof. (Dr.) Monica Yadav, holds a Doctorate from Amity University Haryana and a Law Graduate from Campus Law Centre, Faculty of Law, Delhi University and brings over 15 years of experience in litigation and legal consultancy to her academic career.*

*She is a dynamic academician, skilled communicator, an avid reader & researcher and an effective leader, renowned for her strong analytical prowess, problem-solving abilities and organizational skills.*

*Dr. Yadav specializes in Corporate and Business Laws, with expertise in White-Collar Crime, Taxation Laws, Property Law, Corporate Governance and Business Laws. Her contributions extend to publications in reputable National and International Journals, as well as chapters in Edited Books. Additionally, she has supervised Research Scholars and Post Graduate Students, fostering their academic growth.*

*An esteemed figure in the legal community, Dr. Yadav has served as an invited Speaker, Resource Person and Judge in National and International Moot Court Competitions. She has also played a pivotal role in organizing various prestigious events such as National Moot Court Competitions, International Conferences, Seminars and Workshops, attracting prominent Legal Luminaries.*

# Disclaimer

The contents of this book are personal experiences & life incidents of the author and should be read accordingly. The information provided in this book is intended to be read for informational purpose only. This book is not intended as a substitute for professional medical advice, diagnosis or treatment. The practices, techniques and modalities discussed, including but not limited to Yoga poses, Reiki healing, Chakra healing and Crystals usage, are not meant to diagnose, treat, cure or prevent any medical condition, including thyroid disorders and are merely personal life experiences of the author, by following which, the author kept her thyroid under control without medication.

Individuals using these techniques should do so under the guidance and supervision of qualified healthcare professionals. Every person's health condition is unique and what may be suitable for one individual may not be appropriate for another. It is essential to consult with your doctor/ healthcare advisor before starting any new health regimen, especially if you have pre-existing health conditions or are taking any medication.

The author, publishers and distributors of this book do not assume any liability for any injury, loss or damage incurred by the use or misuse of the information presented herein. Readers are encouraged to use their discretion and seek professional medical advice when making decisions about their health and well-being.

Please consult a doctor before making any health-related decisions. The contents of this book are in no way a substitute for qualified medical opinion. Always consult a specialist or your own doctor for more information. By reading this book, you acknowledge that you have read, understood and agreed to the terms of this disclaimer.

Legal advisors –

**Navit Le-Eagle (OPC) Pvt. Ltd.**
**New Delhi- 110015**

**89 29 188 188**
**89 29 544 544**

# Dedication

To my husband *Navit*,
My cherished family and friends,
Whose love and support know no ends.
For thyroid warriors, brave and strong,
May this book help your journey along.

> *"Embrace Wellness as Your Birthright;*
> *Vibrant Health is within Your Reach."*

# Gratitude

to the **Divine Soul,**

**You are worthy of Vibrant Health**

My deepest & heartfelt gratitude to

my **Gurus, Mentors, Guides** from the realms of

**Yoga**

**Reiki**

**Crystals** and

**Various Holistic Healing Modalities**

for their invaluable support and guidance in navigating and overcoming thyroid issues.

Your wisdom, encouragement and holistic approaches have been instrumental in my healing journey.

Special thanks to the

**Papertowns publishing team**

for their dedication and efforts in the entire publishing process to bring out this book beautifully for bringing awareness to thyroid health and holistic healing modalities.

Together, your contributions have not only empowered me but also inspired others on a path towards wellness and vitality.

# Contents



> *"Health is Your Greatest Asset;*
> *Nurture it with Love, Care and Positivity."*

# Why am I sharing my journey of overcoming Hypothyroidism?

Life with a thyroid condition can be challenging. Thyroid conditions are often misunderstood or overlooked. On a daily basis, individuals might feel overwhelmed or frustrated by persistent fatigue and sluggish metabolism which can drastically affect daily productivity and physical activity, making even routine tasks daunting.

Other physical symptoms like weight management becomes a constant struggle due to the slowed metabolic rate, often leading to frustration and low self-esteem as body image changes.

Cognitive effects like memory lapses and difficulty in concentrating can impair professional performance and personal interactions.

Emotional instability, such as sudden mood swings or unexplained sadness, can further complicate interpersonal relationships and self-perception. The continuous effort to manage symptoms often results in anxiety and may diminish life's pleasures, leading to social withdrawal.

Over time, the chronic nature of any thyroid condition can make one feel isolated, as if battling an invisible illness that others might not fully understand or acknowledge.

Many people suffer silently, fearing judgment or misunderstanding. Some of you might be facing similar issues, feeling discouraged, tired and frustrated due to ongoing thyroid condition.

Discussing my thyroid healing journey and real-life experiences openly may help others in breaking down the isolation. Knowledge and Practice of these details may offer a roadmap for others, providing real-world practical insights and experiences that can guide / encourage them to make better health choices and informed lifestyle adjustments or explore alternative therapies.

Overcoming hypothyroidism is a significant achievement, especially when achieved through holistic practices like Yoga, Reiki, Crystals and Meditation, along with expert guidance and necessary medication.

By sharing my personal journey of overcoming thyroid issues, I wish to create awareness and promote understanding among those who are affected, that they are not alone.

Remember, every healing journey is unique and sharing it can impact lives in unexpected ways. So, if you are considering sharing your own story, go ahead! You never know who might find hope and encouragement through your words.

*Remember, Your Story Matters!!!*

> *Embrace the power within you to overcome challenges and embark on a path of holistic wellness.*

# WHO AM I?

- ❖ Reiki Grandmaster
- ❖ Master Numerologist
- ❖ Numero-Researcher
- ❖ Counsellor
- ❖ Spiritual Guide
- ❖ Crystal Guide & Practitioner
- ❖ Dowsing Practitioner
- ❖ Vedic Switchwords Practitioner
- ❖ Author
- ❖ Zibu Practitioner

- LinkedIn: **@jyotsnaagbansal**
- Instagram: **@JyotsnaaGBansal**
- Google her: **Jyotsnaa G Bansal**
- Mail : **jyotsnaagbansal@gmail.com**

- Speak to her: **+91 98113 43119**

❖ With the core theme of **"Brighten up the Darkest Hours"** of her initiative **"Jyotsnaa The Moonlite",** she caters to domestic as well as International clients - **USA, UK, DUBAI, TANZANIA, GHANA** and many more**.**

She aims to spread the knowledge, importance & impact of our ancient holistic sciences like Yoga, Reiki, Mantras, Meditation, Crystals and Spiritual Healing along with Numerology (impact of our Birthdate Numbers and Name Alphabets) to the common people.

❖ Overcome **HYPOTHYROIDISM** : With her belief, **"Numbers Reveal, Yoga, Reiki, Mantra & Meditation Heal"** she has **overcome HYPOTHYROIDISM.** Today, she is living a perfectly healthy life **minus any medication for Thyroid issues, thanks to Yoga, Reiki & Meditation as well as Mantras & Crystals.**

❖ **First Female Numerologist** to get published her **Numerology Research papers** in **International Journal of Applied Research**, with impact factor (RJIF) 8.4

❖ Contributed as Volunteer in **Vidyanjali** – A School Volunteer Program of ***Department of School Education & Literacy (DoSEL), Ministry of Education, Government of India,*** by providing support for preparation for entrance examinations and competitions in various schools.

❖ Also done **Research work** on **Technical Profession/ Career (Engineering)** with Leading Numerologists.

❖ **First Numerologist** to present the **First Research Paper** on **Global Alliance of Numerologists (GLAON's)** Platform in **<u>FIRST OFFLINE EVENT in April 2023</u>**

❖ Well conversant with different types of numerology like **Chaldean, Surya Ank Jyotish, Vedic-Astro Numerology, Lo-Shu, 9 Star Ki & Pythagoras**. She also guides others through different divinations (Dice, Cowrie, Cards, RamalShastra), Switchwords, Crystals, different symbols & provides counselling as per requirement.

❖ Her articles have been published in renowned astrological journals and magazines.

❖ Also Authored " **Deep Secrets of Name – Advanced Name Numerology based on Chaldean System**" based on real- life case studies & compiled **Anthology with 51 Authors.**

❖ On Reviewer Panel of **MomJunction.com as Name Numerologist**

## <u>Life Path & Occult Journey</u>

❖ Commerce Postgraduate & an MBA (HR).

❖ 13+ yrs' experience in Human Resources (HR) industry as **HEAD Recruitment & Business Development**

❖ Catered to top organisations like **SIEMENS, BLUE STAR, Hero Majestic Group,** as well as **International Clients** and many more.

❖ **Reiki Grandmaster** mentored by **renowned Reiki Grandmasters - Ms. Shanti Malla, Ms. Meenu Minocha, Sqn Ldr (Retd) Ashutosh Bahuguna.**

❖ **Master Teacher** in **Magnified Healing** by **Ms. Shanti Malla** along with **Rev. Kathyrn Anderson & Rev. Gisele King**.

❖ Mentored by **renowned Numerologists**.

❖ Passionate to acquire new skills, learnt **Kathak from Ms. Anjana Singh (Kathak Exponent)** in 2019-2020 from **Prayag Sangeet Samiti, Allahabad.**

❖ Have a keen interest in Art & Craft activities like Madhubani, Embroidery & other handicraft activities.

❖ She practices various Holistic healing modalities along with Numerology, with a desire and passion to help others, with an inclination to bring a positive change in the lives of the concerned persons and in service to humanity.

<u>**Research Papers & Articles by Jyotsnaa G Bansal**</u>
<u>**Presented Conference Papers:**</u>

- **Technical Education/ Career- Engineering** – Based on Vedic-Astro Numerology - **Aug 2022**
- **Alpha-Numeric Analysis of Engineers cum Arbitrators** – Based on Chaldean Name Numerology -  **April 2023**
- **BhagwadGita & World Peace and Harmony** : One day International Seminar at Shri Lal Bahadur Shastri National Sanskrit University, New Delhi -  **Dec 2023**

<u>**Published Articles & Research Papers in International**</u>
<u>**Journals & Magazines:**</u>

- **Aapki Janamtithi ka Rahsay – Ankjyotish ki Drishti se** – Future Samachar, **May 2023**
- Alpha-Numeric Analysis of Engineers cum Arbitrators (Based on Chaldean Name Numerology ) - **International Journal of Applied Research, June 2023**
  https://doi.org/10.22271/allresearch.2023.v9.i6a.10904
- **Your DOB, The Divine Numbers & Colours** – Vedic-Astro. in Yearly Magazine 2023
- Vishv Shanti, Sadbhav aur Samanjasya: Bhagavad Gita ke anusaar - **International Journal of Applied Research, March 2024**
  https://doi.org/10.22271/allresearch.2024.v10.i3c.11764
- "World Peace and Harmony"- Insights from Srimad Bhagavad Gita - **International Journal of Applied Research, April 2024**
  https://doi.org/10.22271/allresearch.2024.v10.i4e.11762
- Decoding Technical Education/Career-Engineering: A study of Planetary Yogs/Combinations as per Vedic Numerology - **International Journal of Applied Research, May 2024**
  https://doi.org/10.22271/allresearch.2024.v10.i5d.11768

# Chapter 1
# Unwarned Meeting with Hypothyroidism

My father, my inspiration, suddenly died in September 2017. Death was unexplainable, sudden and uncalled for. The profound loss threw me in extreme emotional turbulence and grief, shattering my emotional stability. This was the beginning of my dreaded encounter with Thyroid issues, but I was not yet aware of it and of the horrors associated with Thyroid, till I began to experience them.

Life has been like a rollercoaster ride since then, with sudden additional responsibilities and family duties, which caused anxiety and stress to me, beyond my control. Slowly, subtle signs of physical distress began to emerge.

## ❖ Initial struggles and challenges

Next six months were challenging time, as the battle front started with unending fatigue, unexplainable weight gain and hairfall. Initially attributing it to the emotional toll of loss and increased responsibilities, I took it lightly. But gradually, the symptoms intensified as performing daily tasks was becoming difficult and due to emotional heaviness from the raw pain of loss, I was losing clarity of thoughts with the foggy mind.

Concerned about ongoing daily struggles, my husband Navit & myself sought medical advice. After a series of tests and consultations, the diagnosis of Hypothyroidism finally came to light. The medical report revealed elevated levels of TSH.

| Name | : Mrs. JYOTSNA BANSAL | | | | Collected | : 13/3/2018  7:07:00AM |
|---|---|---|---|---|---|---|
| Lab No. | : | Age: Years | Gender: Female | | Received | : 13/3/2018  7:26:30AM |
| A/c Status | : P | Ref By : Dr. | | | Reported | : 13/3/2018  2:52:14PM |
| | | | | | Report Status | : Final |

| Test Name | Results | Units | Bio. Ref. Interval |
|---|---|---|---|
| GLUCOSE, FASTING (F), PLASMA (Hexokinase) | 85.00 | mg/dL | 70.00 - 100.00 |
| TSH, ULTRASENSITIVE, SERUM (CLIA) | 12.291 | uIU/mL | 0.550 - 4.780 |

Interpretation

| REFERENCE GROUP | REFERENCE RANGE in uIU/mL (As per American Thyroid Association) |
|---|---|
| Adult Females(>20 years) | 0.550-4.780 |
| Pregnancy | |
| 1st Trimester | 0.100 - 2.500 |
| 2nd Trimester | 0.200 - 3.000 |
| 3rd Trimester | 0.300 - 3.000 |

*Fig. 1 - TSH Report as on 13 March 2018*

The already present physical and mental toll of grief, coupled with the demanding responsibilities, intensified the challenges of managing hypothyroid symptoms and its effects on my mind and body. What crushed me mentally was the information by the Doctor that it is uncurable and I need to be on medication for the rest of my life.

# Chapter 2

# Understanding Hypothyroidism: Impact on daily life

Since stress is believed to be one of the major factors of Thyroid disorders and after being diagnosed with Hypothyroidism, it became important for me to understand the condition through medical literature and consultations. Not being from Science/ Medical background, there was lack of slightest knowledge about the causes, symptoms etc. of thyroid issues.

As a layman, I started by searching online for information about thyroid issues and hypothyroidism. I looked for reliable sources like medical websites and articles written in easy-to-understand language. I also talked to my doctor and asked questions about the condition, its symptoms, causes and treatments. By combining information from different sources and consulting with my doctor/ physician, I gradually gained a better understanding of hypothyroidism and how it can affect the body. One of the major causes of thyroid issues is believed to be the stressful life conditions prevailing in my life at that time.

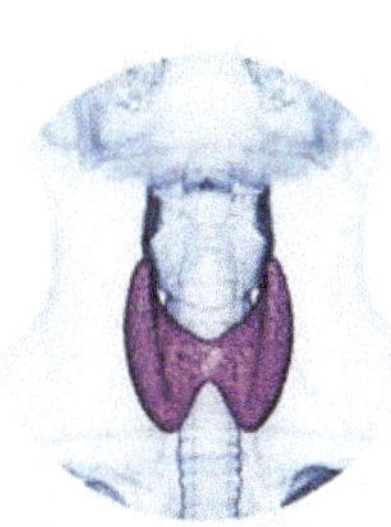

**Thyroid Gland**

The thyroid is a small gland, **like a butterfly**, located in the lower front part of our neck that produces hormones controlling metabolism, energy levels and other functions. **Hypothyroidism happens when the thyroid gland does not make enough hormones to keep the body running normally. It may lead**

**to symptoms like fatigue, weight gain, cold sensitivity and mood changes**. There may be other variable symptoms depending on person to person.

## ❖ Common Causes of Hypothyroidism

From various online resources, I got to know that Hypothyroidism can stem from various factors, such as Autoimmune conditions like Hashimoto's disease, Iodine Deficiency, Thyroid Surgery, certain Medications, Genetic factors, Pregnancy, Age & Gender, Inherited conditions, Hormonal Imbalances and Pituitary Disorders. None of the above factors was present in my case. But the potential causes/ triggers in my scenario appeared to be the Stress due to Loss of Family member, my father. The reasons of my stress were:

a. Emotional trauma and grief from losing a loved one which triggered emotional distress thereby affecting hormone regulation and thyroid function.

b. The emotional & psychological impact of loss which further contributed to mood disorders like depression, which is often associated with hypothyroidism.

Understanding, recognizing and managing potential causes, which in my case were stress & emotional turbulence, was crucial in preventing or addressing hypothyroidism aggravated by emotional trauma.

## ❖ Symptoms

After going through different information sources, I was able to figure out the symptoms some of which I could correlate with my conditions:

1. Fatigue – Overwhelming tiredness started affecting my routine daily life.

2.  Low Energy Levels – lead to lack of enthusiasm & decreased interest in those activities which I enjoyed earlier like Art Craft, Handicraft activities etc.

3.  Weight Gain – At one point, my friend, a boutique owner, asked me if I had joined some gym. That was a disturbing signal for me.

4.  Dry, Itchy Skin – Even after using moisturizing lotions, my skin usually felt itchy & dry.

5.  Thinning hair with Hair Loss – Hypothyroidism often leads to common symptoms of hair thinning and loss due to the slowed metabolism.

6.  Brittle nails – Nails started breaking frequently over a period of time.

7.  Forgetfulness – I used to forget small things while performing daily life routine functions. This started making me irritated most of the time.

8.  Sadness / Depressive thoughts – I used to have disturbing thoughts that made me feel sad, depressive about life.

9.  Puffy face, Hoarse Voice – Due to reduced thyroid levels, my face especially around the eyes and cheeks looked puffy/ swollen

10. Concentration issues, Anxiety – Focusing on any task was becoming increasingly difficult.

11. Constipation – The erratic thyroid levels disturbed the digestion process, ultimately leading to constipation.

12. Irregular Menstrual Cycle – Overall imbalance in hormones resulted in irregular menstrual cycles, making me more anxious.

However, my cholesterol levels and Heart rate were under control. But I started getting annoyed easily as feelings of worry constantly plagued me. At times, I avoided social interactions, wanted to be alone.

Overall, the symptoms significantly impaired daily functioning, work performance, relationships and overall well-being.

With the consistent difficulties in daily life, we decided to seek medical advice & consultation. Based on our detailed discussions, the doctor advised blood tests to measure levels of Thyroid Hormones. There are the 3 key medical tests used for diagnosing thyroid disorders, viz Thyroid Stimulating Hormone (TSH) Test, T4 (Thyroxine) and T3 (Triiodothyronine) Test.

I was advised TSH test. As the best way to initially test thyroid function is to measure the TSH (Thyroid Stimulating Hormone) level in the blood sample.

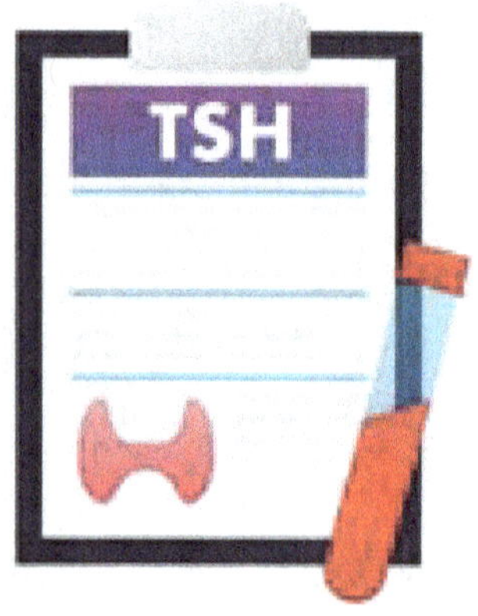


TSH is a hormone produced by the pituitary gland that signals the thyroid gland to produce thyroid hormones (T4 and T3). **High TSH levels** typically indicate hypothyroidism, while low levels may suggest hyperthyroidism. This is the most important and sensitive test for hypothyroidism. **An abnormally high TSH means hypothyroidism: the thyroid gland is not making enough thyroid hormone.**

The medical reports revealed alarmingly elevated levels of TSH confirming Hypothyroidism.

The immediate next step was to determine the most suitable treatment plan based on the specific conditions, symptoms and overall health status.

So, conventional treatment involving thyroid specific medicines was suggested. The goal of treatment was to restore normal thyroid hormone levels in the body. This treatment was effective in managing symptoms such as fatigue, weight gain and depression associated with hypothyroidism.

From the information gathered from various online resources, we knew that patients with hypothyroidism usually require lifelong treatment and regular follow-up appointments with physician/ consulting doctor to ensure optimal thyroid hormone levels and overall well-being. However, one significant and disturbing limitation was the need for lifelong medication. Me and Navit, both were not comfortable with the very same idea.

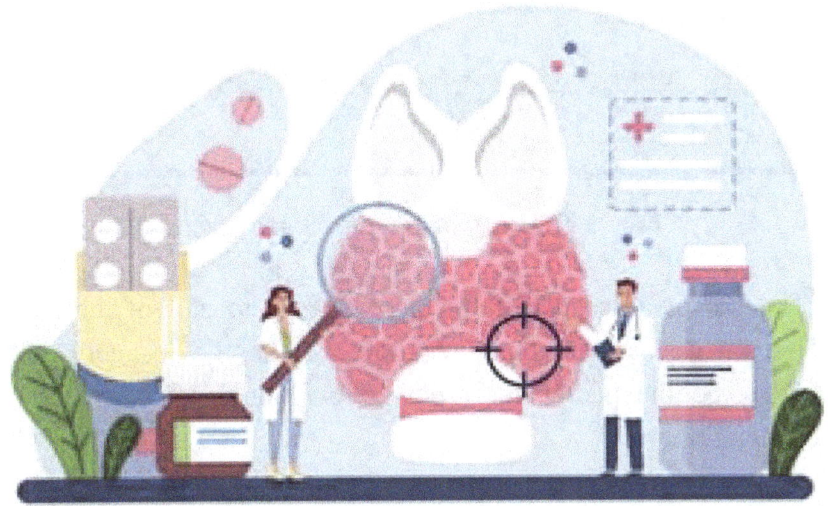

Another alarming information was about the potential side effects from thyroid hormone related medication, such as heart palpitations, insomnia or excessive sweating.

However, to control the situation at hand, I started taking prescribed medicines and continued for 2 months. After 2 months, again TSH test was conducted. The medical reports showed the thyroid levels within the permissible range.

The doctor advised to reduce the dosage to half of the initially suggested. I was worried that every few months, the dosage was to be changed as per the medical test reports. How long this was going to take to get back to normal?

# Chapter 3

# Turning Point: Discovery of Alternative Healing Modalities

At this crucial point, Navit & me took a huge chance. Instead of reducing the dosage, I stopped the medicines and started seeking alternatives to conventional treatments. Based on my situation at that time, I shifted to Homeopathic medicines in consultation with Homeopathic physician. I continued the homeopathic medicines for next 3 months along with some dietary changes and precautions. Meanwhile, I was also searching for holistic healing modalities and self-care regimen to regulate thyroid hormones and overall physical, mental and emotional well-being.

This pivotal phase marked the beginning of a transformative journey, where I turned to Yoga, recognizing the Mind-Body connection. Simultaneously, I explored the energy of self-healing practice of Reiki, focusing on the Throat Chakra more and balancing the other chakras. Reiki & Yoga sessions helped me in reducing stress and anxiety.

Using crystals in different forms also helped in balancing the hormones and calming the mind and reducing the stress factor. I will discuss about specific crystals which I used for myself, in coming chapter. To strengthen the healing, I started specific Mantra chanting which helped me align my vibrational energy and promoted mindfulness.

I continued with this integrative holistic approach for few months, where self-care, holistic practices and inner strength became guiding lights through the darkest of times. In general, Thyroid patients are advised to undergo regular blood test to monitor thyroid levels to maintain a healthy lifestyle. So, a blood test was done again.

The reports this time came as a pleasant surprise as the TSH levels were within the permissible range. Navit & me, both were relieved, as we took a chance to discontinue the conventional medicines and shifted to alternative medicine & modalities. And it paid off very well.

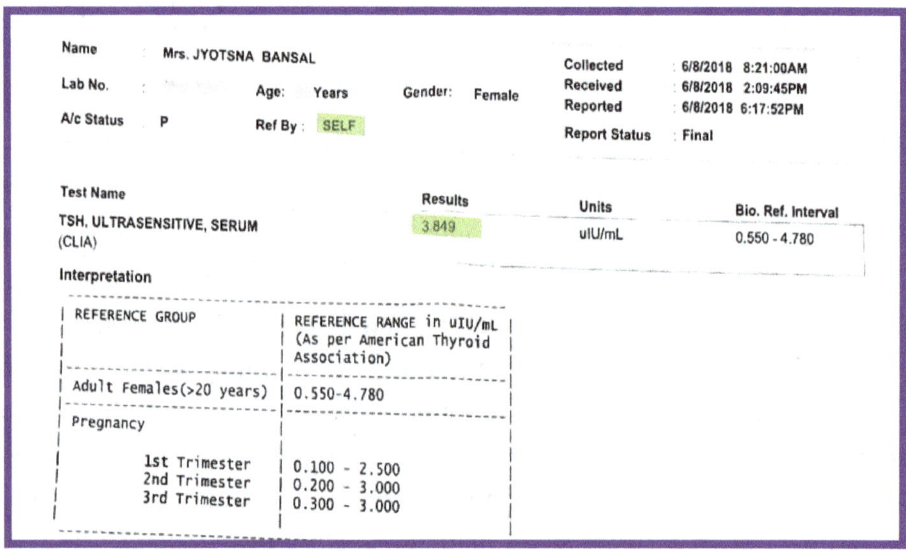

Fig. 3 TSH Report as on 6 Aug 2018

Now, there was a ray of hope….that by continuing the above approach, I could at least ward off the potential risk of side effects associated with the thyroid medication. However, the TSH this time increased from the last report, but still it was in the permissible range. That was a big satisfaction for me.

With this, I also decided to get blood tests done at regular intervals, to keep a check on TSH levels. So, following same practice, after few months, got another TSH test done which gave positive results…

| Name | : Mrs. JYOTSNA BANSAL | | | Collected | : 11/12/2018 7:44:00AM |
|---|---|---|---|---|---|
| Lab No. | : | Age: Years | Gender: Female | Received | : 11/12/2018 7:57:23AM |
| | | | | Reported | : 11/12/2018 2:54:58PM |
| A/c Status | : P | Ref By : SELF | | Report Status | : Final |

| Test Name | Results | Units | Bio. Ref. Interval |
|---|---|---|---|
| TSH, ULTRASENSITIVE, SERUM (CLIA) | 4.714 | uIU/mL | 0.550 - 4.780 |

Interpretation

| REFERENCE GROUP | REFERENCE RANGE in uIU/mL (As per American Thyroid Association) |
|---|---|
| Adult Females(>20 years) | 0.550-4.780 |
| Pregnancy | |
| 1st Trimester | 0.100 - 2.500 |
| 2nd Trimester | 0.200 - 3.000 |
| 3rd Trimester | 0.300 - 3.000 |

**Fig. 4 TSH Report as on 11 Dec 2018**

I decided to follow the same course of action and get the blood test done annually. Every subsequent test was boosting my self- confidence and my belief in holistic healing practices.

Meanwhile, I also started learning Kathak from Jun-July 2019. The rhythmic footwork and intricate movements boost metabolism, helping to regulate thyroid function. This further strengthened muscles, improved my flexibility, posture, body rhythm and reduced stress.

**My learning:** *"Dance and Yoga: different paths, same destination of harmony and self-discovery. Yoga grounds us, dance liberates us, together they elevate us."*

In the last quarter of 2019, I also discontinued the homeopathic medicines (after consulting the doctor) as most of the symptoms subsided by that time and my life was back on healthy track. After few months, in Feb 2020, got the TSH test done to keep a check on the TSH levels.

And this time, as I kept my fingers crossed with my utmost belief in the alternative holistic healing modalities, the medical reports confirmed that I was on the right path to vibrant health. The TSH levels were again in the permissible range.

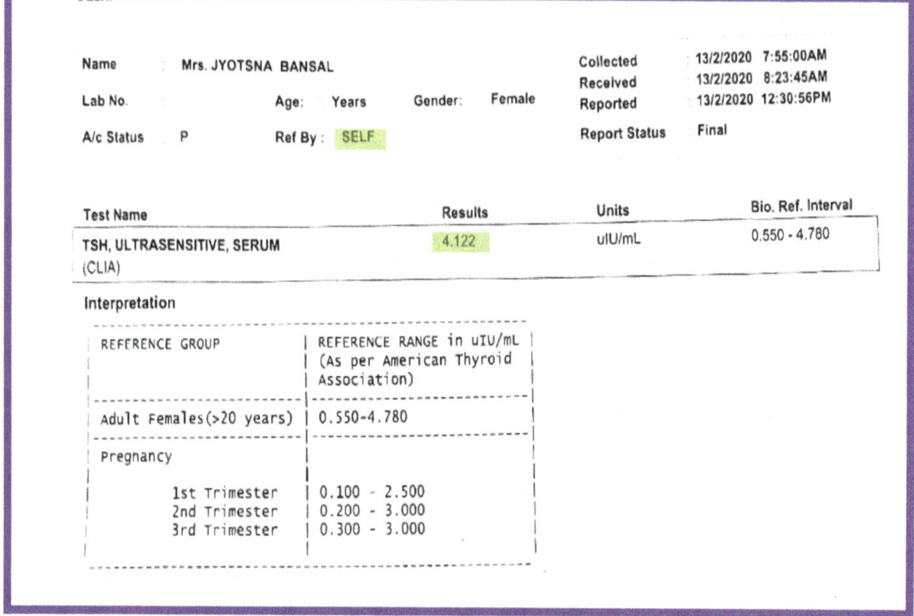

*Fig. 5 TSH Report as on 13 Feb 2020*

This was the last report (Fig 5) just before the Covid Pandemic hit the world. During next few months, I followed my earlier practices for overall health well-being.

When the dust settled down & things started getting back to normal, I felt a sense of relief and optimism. As during all those years, I was off the medication for thyroid issues and was diligently following alternative and holistic healing modalities which transformed my overall well-being.

The latest TSH test reports (conducted on 10 June 2023) confirmed the significance of integrative approach of holistic healing practices combining Yoga, Reiki, Crystals, Mantra and Meditation and amazing transformative healing energies.

| PATIENT NAME | :Mrs. JYOTSNAA | AGE/SEX | : . . YRS / F |
| LAB SERIAL NO | : ----------- | REGISTERED | :10-Jun-2023 08:08AM |
| REFERRED BY | :Dr. SELF | COLLECTED | :10-Jun-2023 01:21PM |
| SAM.'LE . | :-- ----- | REPORTED | :10-Jun-2023 03:17PM |

### IMMUNOLOGY

| Test Name | Result | Bio. Ref. Range | Method |
| --- | --- | --- | --- |
| THYROID STIMULATING HORMONE[TSH] | 2.51 uIu/ml | 0.35-4.94 | CMIA |

**Note :**

TSH levels are subject to circadian variation, rising several hours before the onset of sleep and reaching peak levels between 11 PM to 6AM. Lowest concentrations are observed during the afternoon. There can be an approximate 50%, variation in levels of TSH. Hence the time of sampling has influence on the measured serum TSH concentrations.

In pregnancy due to hormonal changes, the levels of $T_3$ & $T_4$ increase by about 50%. As a result, the normal TSH levels during pregnancy are less than the non pregnant levels.

*Fig. 6 - TSH Report as on 10 Jun 2023*

# Chapter 4

# Exploring Alternative Healing Modalities

## Holistic Approach:

In addition to medication, physician/ consulting doctors often advise patients to maintain a healthy lifestyle, including a balanced diet, regular exercise, stress management and adequate sleep.

Now, that we were ready to explore the alternative healing modalities, addressing emotional and mental health aspects also became crucial for the holistic and comprehensive approach to hypothyroidism care. Hypothyroidism is a condition that casts a shadow over daily life with its symptoms of fatigue, weight gain and emotional turbulence.

Navit was my pillar of strength and confidence, throughout this healing journey as at times, I started feeling emotionally low and energy levels dipped. With the constant motivation, regular reminders to follow routines and the unwavering support of my husband, Adv. Navit Bansal, I started my healing journey.

# Yoga for Thyroid Health

Yoga offers a holistic approach to managing thyroid disorders, integrating gentle postures with mindful breathing to promote hormonal balance and overall wellness.

Regular Yoga practice can help correct thyroid problems effectively. Several Yoga poses or asanas stimulate blood flow to the thyroid glands and enhance energy flow and stretch & strengthen the neck. Consistently practicing relevant Yoga poses proves to be an effective natural remedy for those seeking to harmonize their body's functions, flexibility, posture and improve thyroid health.

Once you have a Thyroid condition, Yoga cannot replace medication completely but can reduce the medication dependency considerably.

Initially I started with daily 5-7 minutes of Yoga, focusing on poses that activate the throat area, enhancing thyroid function. Gradually, I increased the time up to 20 minutes daily.

Here I am sharing the poses in the sequence that I followed. Adding some or all of these yoga poses to your daily routine may help to improve your thyroid function and regulate thyroid hormones by stimulating the thyroid gland. These yoga poses also help in strengthening muscles and also reducing effects of hypothyroidism on the body.

In the beginning, it was not easy to remember all the poses, but slowly, with practice it became routine.

<u>**My tip:**</u>

Be gentle and easy with yourself. Always listen to your body. Do what feels best on a daily basis. Try to do at least a little bit of yoga each day You don't have to do all of the poses in one session, you can try a pose or two on a single day. You can adjust or modify the poses to suit your needs. Also, if you feel ok, you can do these yoga poses coupled with Pranayama techniques – breathing exercises (e.g., Ujjayi breath, Kapalbhati, alternate nostril breathing), under expert's guidance & supervision. However, I sticked to Yoga poses only.

*Word of caution:* When should thyroid patients avoid doing yoga?

Few reasons to refrain from doing yoga:

- When the doctor advises against it.

- Persons with severe hyperthyroidism/ hypothyroidism symptoms.

- Persons with extreme joint pain.

- Persons with other pre-existing medical conditions.

Disclaimer: The Yoga poses demonstrated here are for knowledge purpose only which author followed personally as per her condition. They are not a substitute for professional instruction or medical advice. It is essential to consult with a qualified yoga instructor or physician/ consulting doctor before attempting any yoga pose, especially if you have any pre-existing medical conditions, physical limitations or concerns about your health. The author and publishers of this content disclaim any liability for injuries or damages arising from the use of these yoga poses. Practice at your own risk and listen to your body's limitations and signals at all times.

## 1. Balasana (Child Pose)

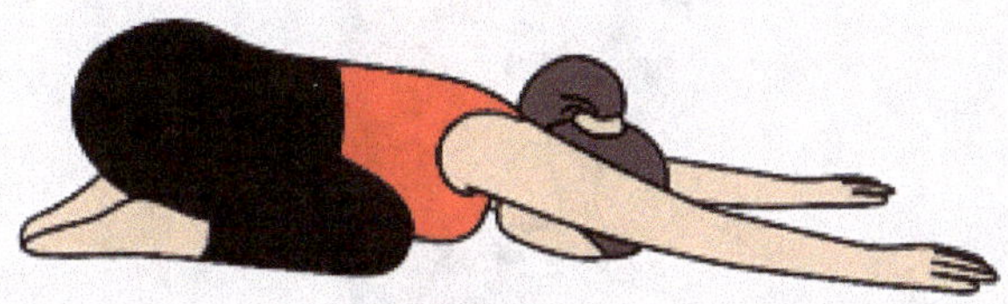

- Relieves stress and fatigue
- Stimulates the thyroid gland, improves its functioning
- Helps in relaxation and calming the nervous system
- Improves blood circulation and aids in digestion

 **Balasana (Child Yoga Pose)**

## 2. Marjaryasana (Cat-Cow Pose)

- Promotes hormonal balance
- Massages the thyroid & parathyroid glands
- Enhances flexibility in the spine and improves posture
- Improves digestion and metabolism
- Relieves tension in the back and neck

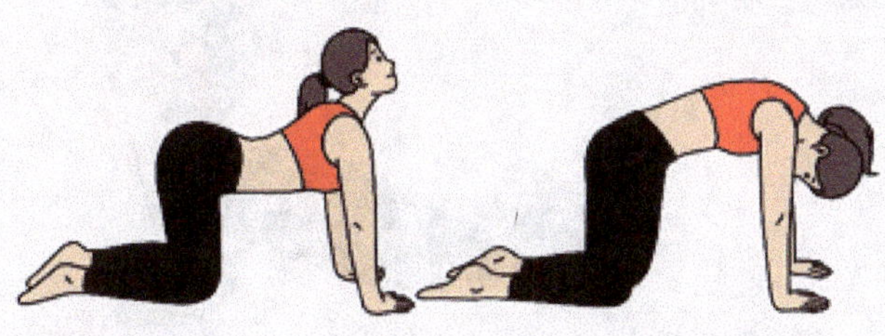 **Marjaryasana (Cat-Cow Pose)**

## 3.  Ustrasana (Camel Pose)

- Increases the blood circulation in thyroid glands
- Improves hormonal balance
- Stretches the front of the body, including the neck and chest
- Improves posture and spinal flexibility
- Boosts energy levels and reduces fatigue

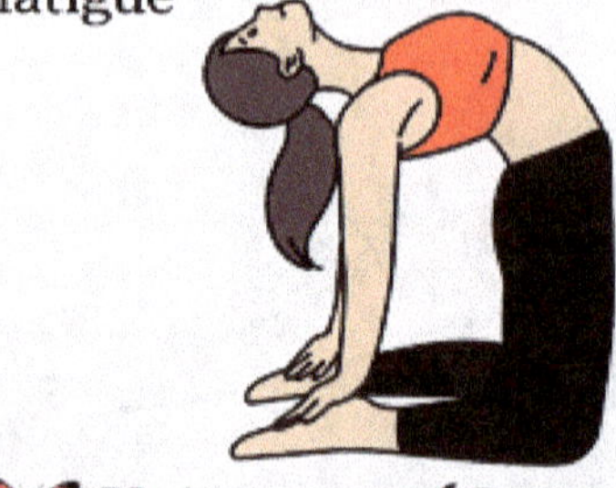

**Ustrasana (Camel Pose)**

## 4.  Bhujangasana (Cobra Pose)

- Stretches neck & throat region and improves circulation
- Strengthens the back muscles
- Stimulates the thyroid gland
- Opens up the chest and improves lung capacity
- Reduces stress

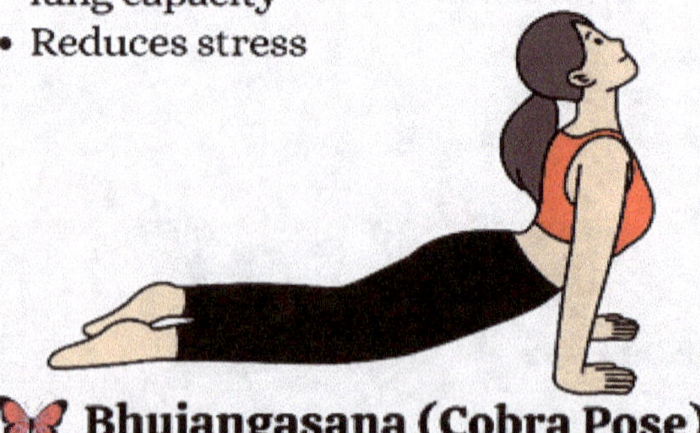

**Bhujangasana (Cobra Pose)**

## 5. Dhanurasana (Bow Pose)

- Stimulates the thyroid gland and improves its functioning
- Strengthens the back muscles and improves posture
- Improves metabolism
- Aids in weight management
- Increases energy levels

**Dhanurasana (Bow Pose)**

## 6. Setu Bandhasana (Bridge Pose )

- Improves blood circulation in the thyroid glands
- Stretches the neck and chest muscles
- Reduces tension and promotes relaxation
- Helps in improving digestion and metabolism
- Helps in relieving stress and anxiety

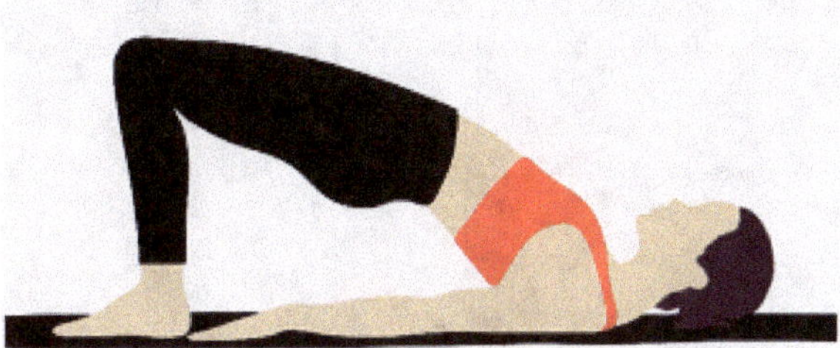

**Setu Bandhasana (Bridge Pose)**

### 7. Matasyasana (Fish Pose)

- Stimulates the thyroid gland and improves its functioning
- Stretches the neck and throat muscles, enhancing thyroid health
- Opens up the chest and improves breathing
- Relieves fatigue and promotes relaxation

**Matsyasana (Fish Pose)**

### 8. Viparita Karani (Legs up the Wall Pose)

- Relieves tension in the legs and lower back
- Promotes relaxation and reduces stress
- Improves blood circulation
- Calms the nervous system and improves sleep quality

**Viparita Karani (Legs up the Wall Pose)**

## 9. Sarvangasana (Shoulder Stand)

- Stimulates the thyroid gland and improves its functioning.
- Enhances blood flow to the neck and head region
- Strengthens the shoulders, arms, and core muscles
- Relieves stress and fatigue

**Sarvangasana (Shoulder Stand)**

## 10. Halasana (Plow Pose)

- Stimulates the thyroid gland and improves hormonal balance
- Stretches the back and neck muscles, improving flexibility
- Improves digestion and metabolism, supporting overall health
- Relieves stress and fatigue, promoting relaxation and well-being

**Halasana (Plow Pose)**

Apart from the above yoga poses, I also performed following poses for better flexibility, improved digestion & metabolism and to boost my energy levels:

1. Trikonasana (Triangle Pose)

2. Paadhastasana Uttansana (Standing Forward Bend)

3. Paschimotansana (Seated Forward Bend)

4. Utkata Konasana (Goddess Squat)

5. Vrikshasana (Tree Pose)

6. Baddha Konasana (Butterfly pose)

7. Malasana (Garland Pose)

8. Pawanmuktasana (Wind Release Pose)

9. Shava Udarakarshanasana (Universal Spinal Twist)

# Chapter 5
# The Power of Reiki Healing

*Expressing heartfelt gratitude to Reiki Gurus,*
**Mrs. Shanti Malla**, *Founder - Atma Jagriti*
*(Research, Training & Healing Foundation)*
**Mrs. Meenu Minocha,** *Reiki Grandmaster, Holistic Practitioner*
**Sq. Leader Ashutosh Bahuguna,** *Reiki Grandmaster,*
*Founder – BetterAll*
*Your wisdom, teachings & guidance has transformed my healing journey and life.*

## What is Reiki?

The word Reiki is made of two Japanese words - **Rei** which means "Universal" and **Ki** which is "Life Energy". So, Reiki is actually **"Universal Life Energy."**

Reiki is an ancient Japanese healing technique which is simple, natural and safe method of spiritual healing, stress reduction and relaxation. It is a hands-on healing technique, which involves channeling energy through the hands. **Dr. Mikao Usui** (Usui Sensei) is the founder of the Reiki System of Healing, which was further propagated by **Dr. Chujiro Hayashi** and **Mrs. Hawayo Takata**.

**Dr. Mikao Usui**
15 Aug 1865 – 9 Mar 1926

**Dr. Chujiro Hayashi**
15 Sep 1880 – 11 May 1940

**Mrs. Hawayo Takata**
24 Dec 1900 – 11 Dec 1980

The following are the 5 Principles (Precepts) of Reiki.

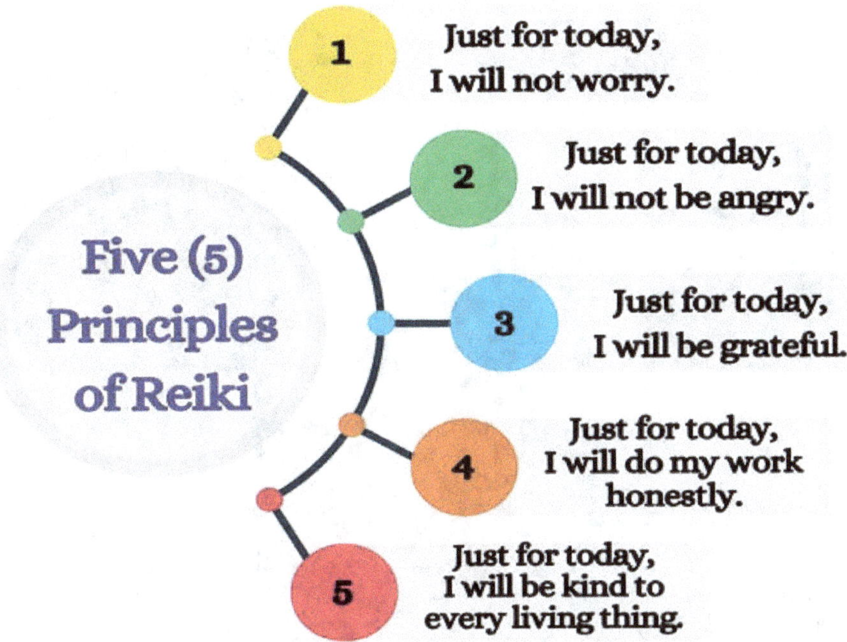


Reiki is used for physical, emotional and mental healing and it can be practiced by anyone irrespective of age, gender, religion, caste or nationality. Reiki can be practiced in person or at a distance. This just needs the Attunement from the qualified Reiki Master or Reiki Grandmaster. It can complement medical treatments but is not a replacement.

Being a Reiki practitioner, I knew the basic details of energy healing and 7 major chakras in our body. So, I customized my healing sessions to focus on the relevant chakras to handle the health issues at hand.

While following my yoga routine, I combined it with the self-healing practice of Reiki. Regular Reiki sessions facilitated energy flow, addressing the energetic imbalances contributing to hypothyroidism.

Self-healing sessions helped a lot and a significant improvement in my energy levels and overall well-being was visible. This further strengthened my belief in Reiki, which, later on, led me to learn Reiki up to the **Grandmaster level**.

During the healing sessions, major focus was on the throat chakra (which is the Fifth chakra, *Vishuddhi or Vishuddha*) & related chakras, which corresponds to the thyroid gland. This process not only supported my physical well-being but also promoted emotional healing, reducing stress and anxiety, which are known to aggravate Thyroid issues.

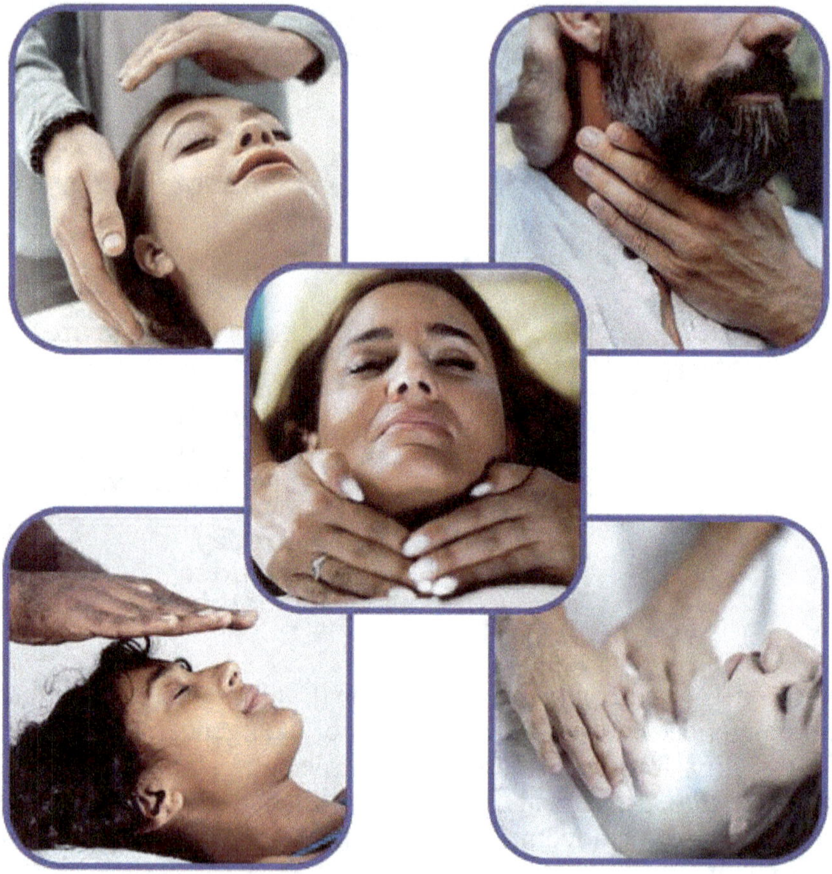

Disclaimer: The information provided in this book regarding Crystals, Chakra Healing, Mantras and Guided Meditation, is for knowledge purposes only. They are not intended as a substitute for professional medical advice, diagnosis or treatment. Crystals, Chakra healing techniques, Mantras and meditation should be used /practiced responsibly under the guidance of a qualified practitioner/ instructor/ mentor. Individual experiences with these practices can differ and individual results may vary and there are no guarantees of specific outcomes  or the effectiveness of crystal healing techniques. The author and publishers of this content disclaim any liability for the use or misuse of chakra healing practices, mantras and guided meditation techniques. It is highly recommended to consult with an expert instructor/ mentor or qualified practitioner before starting any new spiritual or wellness practice or incorporating crystal healing into your wellness routine

## "Energy Flows where Intention goes."

# Chapter 6
# Mantra & Meditation Practices

While practicing Reiki self-healing, the emphasis is also on chakra healing in our body.

Chakras are energy centers in the human body that play a crucial role in our physical, emotional and spiritual well-being. There are seven main chakras, each located along the spine, starting from the base and extending to the crown of the head. Each chakra is associated with specific organs, emotions and spiritual aspects.

The seven main chakras are :

1. Root or Muladhara Chakra

2. Sacral or Swadhishtana Chakra

3. Solar Plexus or Manipura Chakra

4. Heart or Anahata Chakra

5. Throat or Vishuddha Chakra

6. Third Eye or Ajna Chakra

7. Crown or Sahasrara Chakra

When chakras are balanced, energy flows smoothly, keeping us healthy and happy. Imbalances in chakras can lead to physical ailments, emotional disturbances and spiritual disconnect or disconnect from self.

Each Chakra has its own corresponding Beej mantra that helps to activate and balance its energy. **"Beej"** means seed and these seed mantras are believed to hold the essence of the chakra's energy. So, Chakra Beej mantras are sacred seed sounds associated with the seven primary and main chakras in the human energy system. The Beej mantras are:

1. Root Chakra (Muladhara): "**Lam**"

2. Sacral Chakra (Swadhishtana): "**Vam**"

3. Solar Plexus Chakra (Manipura): "**Ram**"

4. Heart Chakra (Anahata): "**Yam**"

5. Throat Chakra (Vishuddha): "**Ham**"

6. Third Eye Chakra (Ajna): "**Om**"

7. Crown Chakra (Sahasrara): "**Aum**"

Chanting these mantras helps to clear energy blockages. Also, it can help activate, balance and harmonize the energy of each chakra, which further promotes physical, emotional and spiritual well-being.

So, while practicing self-healing sessions of Reiki, with the focus on Throat chakra, I also followed chanting of Throat chakra's Beej mantra - "Ham".

This overall practice took the shape of customized meditation. Since stress is believed to be one of the major factors of thyroid disorders, self-healing and meditation keep the mind calm, relaxed and alleviates everyday stress.

Gradually, Mantra chanting became a daily ritual. I started chanting the '**Gayatri Mantra**' and '**Maha Mrityunjaya Mantra**' too, which are specifically known for their healing vibrations. Before chanting mantras, I set my intentions that thyroid gland is getting healed and positive vibrations are strengthening my immune system. These mantras also created an environment for healing.

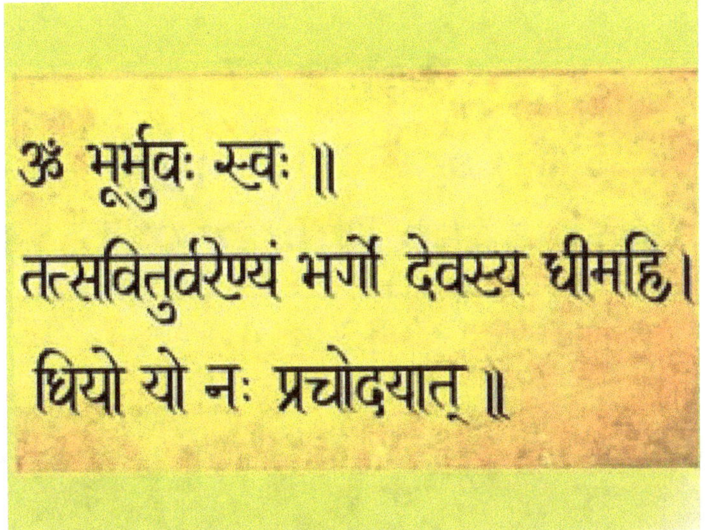

This overall practice deepened my mind-body connection which helped significantly in reducing stress levels. The positive vibrations of chanting helped in enhancing my body's natural healing capabilities.

There are certain other techniques for stress management (discussed further), which one can use as per his/ her own choice or convenience.

# Chapter 7
# Crystal Therapy: Harnessing the Energy of Crystals

*(1943- 2021)*
*Source: FB Page- Crystal Judy Hall*

*In loving memory of Judy Hall, a brilliant crystal expert, whose profound knowledge and passion for crystals transformed countless lives. Judy's dedication to the study of art and science of crystals continues to inspire and guide us. This knowledge-sharing content is dedicated to her enduring legacy, honoring her invaluable contributions and the inspiration she provided. Thank you, Judy, for your invaluable wisdom and your extraordinary gift to the world.*

Crystals are natural mineral formations with unique geometric structures, special shapes and vibrations. They are believed to possess healing properties due to their ability to emit stable, consistent vibrations that can influence the energy around them. Each type of Crystal has specific healing properties: for example, Amethyst is known for calming and enhancing spiritual awareness, Rose Quartz promotes love and emotional healing and Citrine is associated with abundance and positivity.

These vibrations of crystals can help balance physical, emotional and spiritual energies, promoting overall well-being and healing. Crystal Practitioners often utilize crystals in meditation, energy healing practices and as part of their daily wellness routines.

For using crystals, it is better if you know Reiki because crystals need to be purified, programmed, de-programmed, charged with positive vibes and intentions according to our requirements. Although one can use crystals without knowing Reiki, the symbols used in different Reiki levels enhance the healing effect of the crystals.

While learning Reiki I also got to know about amazing healing power of crystals as it was part of Reiki teachings. So, I studied bit more about crystals that could help heal thyroid gland back to normal.

## Types of Crystals beneficial for Thyroid health

I got to know about lot of throat chakra stones, some of which are Aquamarine, Lapis Lazuli, Labradorite, Turquoise, Amazonite, Sodalite, Blue Lace Agate, Angelite, Blue Apatite, Chrysocolla, Blue Chalcedony, Blue Kyanite, Celestite, Azurite, Larimar and many more. They help to remove blockages in the throat and facilitate clear and open communication.

After confirming from my guru and crystal experts, I narrowed down on Clear Quartz, Labradorite, Lapis Lazuli, Turquoise, all related to Throat Chakra.

I used Lapis Lazuli as tumble stone and bracelet, Turquoise as pendant, Clear Quartz as tumble stone and kept Labradorite by my bedside. (Crystals come in different forms: - Pencil (Wand), Tumble stones, Raw Stones, Clusters, Cubes, Spheres, Heart shape, Pyramids, Geodes, also in jewelry form like- bracelet, pendant, ear-rings, Rings. You can use any form you feel resonated with.)

### 1. Lapis Lazuli- Stone of Communication & Wisdom

Lapis Lazuli

It balances the throat chakra and helps in emotional healing and communication. It is also linked to Third-Eye Chakra & enhances psychic abilities and gives clear perspectives. This stone harmonizes the physical, emotional, mental and spiritual levels. It helps in expressing feelings and emotions . It quickly releases stress, bringing deep peace and clarity. It helps in expressing your own opinions and harmonizes conflict by resolving emotional issues.

Putting the Reiki-charged Lapis Lazuli on Throat Chakra while lying down further helps in relaxation & helps the endocrine system and thyroid glands. Also, wearing as a bracelet also helps in calming the restless mind and clears confusion.

To care for Lapis Lazuli, it is recommended to cleanse it under running water, charge it by the moonlight and keep it away from harsh chemicals to preserve its vibrant blue hue and potent energies.

## 2. Labradorite – Mystical Stone of Magic & Transformation

Labradorite strengthens faith in the self and trust in the universe. it calms an overactive mind, relieves stress and regulates metabolism. Labradorite is connected to the throat chakra and the third eye chakra. It also balances hormones. It boosts your psychic powers and deepens intuition. Labradorite has many healing properties which clear blockages in the throat chakra and the third eye chakra.

**Labradorite**

Labradorite can be cleansed by running it under water, can be charged by leaving it in moonlight or leave it with charging crystals like Selenite and Clear Quartz. Smudging with Sage or Palo Santo is also a great way to clear any stagnant energy.

## 3. Turquoise – Mystical Stone of Hope, Protection & Good Luck

**Tumbled**

**Polished**

**Turquoise**

Turquoise is a most efficient healer protective stone. It enhances communication. Turquoise balances and aligns all the chakras and helps in purification by dispelling negative energy. It also strengthens the immune system.

Turquoise stabilizes mood swings and brings calmness. It is an excellent stone for depression or fatigue. It is especially useful for healing throat chakra blockages as it possesses the healing power for throat & respiratory organ-related issues. It is also called the **Purification Stone**. It purifies the Aura on all levels.

Turquoise can be cleansed gently with warm soapy water and a soft-bristled brush. It can be charged by smudging with Sage or Palo Santo.

## 4. Clear Quartz – Universal Crystal, Master Healer

Clear quartz works on all levels as it is the most powerful healing and energy amplifier, also referred to as "**Master Healer.**" It is the easiest crystal to program and may be used for many purposes. It knows exactly what to do with all that excess energy running around and where to channel it to bring out the best results.

Clear Quartz Crystal is a powerful protective stone that harmonizes and balances universal energy. It is known for its ability to clear negative thoughts, blockages, heal any condition, improve the immune system, boost the energy levels and enhance higher spiritual receptiveness.

Clear quartz aids in spiritual growth, healing and manifesting goals by either wearing it, meditating with it or placing it in the living spaces.

Clear quartz should be cleansed and recharged regularly, which can be done by keeping it under running water, by smudging with sage, or placing it on a selenite charging plate and charging can be done by placing it in sunlight or moonlight.

# Cleansing Crystals

Cleansing crystals is essential to maintain their healing and energetic properties. Over time, crystals absorb negative energies and impurities from their surroundings, which can diminish their effectiveness. Regular cleansing removes these accumulated energies and helps in restoring the crystals' natural vibrations. Regular cleansing also enhances their ability to promote physical, emotional and spiritual healing and positive energy.

After cleansing, it is important to charge and program the crystals for further use.

**How to cleanse crystals for healing?**

_My Tip:_ Those who know Reiki, should use Reiki symbols for cleansing & charging process as the symbols enhance the healing power of the crystals.

There are several methods for cleansing the crystals, but not every method can be used for every crystal. As some crystals are soft, some are hard, not all crystals can handle salt water, or sunlight or some other method.

Some commonly used methods are:

1. **Running Water:** Hold the crystal under natural running water or a tap or stream for a few minutes. Visualize that all the negative energy is being washed away with the running water.

2. **Saltwater:** Soak the crystal in saltwater overnight, then rinse and dry it. Be cautious with porous stones.

3. **Sunlight or Moonlight:** This is the simplest and safest method. Place the crystal in sunlight for a few hours or moonlight overnight to recharge its energy. Please check whether the crystal can be put in sunlight or not.

4. **Smudging:** Pass the crystal through the smoke of burning sage, Palo Santo, or incense to remove negative energy.

5. **Earth:** Bury the crystal in soil for 24 hours to reconnect it with earth's natural energy. After removing from earth/ soil, clean it and make sure that no soil/ earth particles are left behind.

6. **Visualization**: Hold the crystal and visualize a bright white light surrounding it, purifying its energy.

7. **Reiki:** Use Reiki energy to cleanse it. Place your crystals in your palm and draw the first symbol- **Cho Ku Rei** over the crystal. Send healing energy with your intention that negative energy is being removed from the crystal.

8. **Bell Sound or Singing Bowl:** Use a singing bowl, or bells to cleanse the crystals with sound vibrations.

9. **Breath**: Breathe deeply and exhale sharply over the crystal with the intention to clear away negative energies. Do it thrice atleast.

10. **Rain**: Leave the crystal outside during a rain shower to cleanse it with natural water. Avoid prolonged exposure to harsh weather.

11. **Selenite Plate**: Selenite is a self-cleansing crystal and is referred as **"Universal Stone Cleanser."** Simply place the crystal on a selenite plate or slab for several hours to clear negative energies.

## Charging Crystals

After cleansing, charging crystals with divine energy and positive intentions enhances their healing properties. Crystals, like kids, have unique characteristics and special qualities. Crystals are just like a small kid, whom you cleanse/ purify, then charge with positive energy & guide (program) them for your specific goal achievements. So, they also need to be cared and pampered like small kids. When properly cared for, crystals, like children, can bring joy, healing and positive energy into our lives. Their energy grows and becomes more powerful with proper care and positive intentions.

**How to charge crystals for healing?**

*My Tip:* Reiki practitioners can charge and program crystals simultaneously by giving Reiki to the crystal and setting positive intentions.

There are few simple and commonly used methods for charging as mentioned below:

1. **Reiki**: Use Reiki energy and symbols to charge the crystals. Place your hands over the crystal and channelize universal life force energy into it. Reiki charging is simple, gentle and powerful. This method can be used for any crystal. It enhances the crystal's natural vibrations and effectiveness.

2. **Prayers & Mantras**: Hold the crystals and say any prayer that ou feel connected with, to bless and charge the crystals with their energy. Any mantra, that resonates with your current requirement or wish, can also be chanted to charge the crystals.

3. **Crystal Grid**: Place the crystal in a crystal grid designed for charging, with other crystals arranged in a specific pattern to amplify the energy.

4. **Moonlight** : Place the crystal under moonlight. Imagine the light filling the crystal with divine energy. Visualize positive intentions entering the crystal. This charging process boosts the crystal's natural power as Moonlight provides calm, soothing energy. This simple practice strengthens the crystal's energy with positive intentions.

5. **Affirmations**: Hold the crystal and speak or think positive statements. Say affirmations such as "I charge this crystal with love and healing energy." Affirmations align the crystal with your goals. It's a simple way to boost the crystal's effectiveness and healing properties.

6. **Incense Smoke**: After cleansing the crystal, light an incense. Hold the crystal in the smoke. Visualize divine energy filling the crystal. Think or say positive intentions, like "I charge this crystal with

love." The incense smoke purifies and charges the crystal. This method enhances the crystal's healing power with positive energy.

# Programming Crystals

Programming crystals means setting specific goals or intentions for them. Programming is a powerful practice that helps direct the crystal's energy toward achieving specific, positive results in our life. It boosts the crystal's power.

**How to program crystals for healing?**

After cleansing, hold the crystal in your hand, close your eyes and focus on your intention. Clearly state or visualize what you want the crystal to support, such as healing, protection, or love.

Just like charging methods, some of these can be used for programming too:

1.  **Reiki**: Place the crystal in one hand and the dominant hand over it. Use Reiki energy and symbols (whichever you feel comfortable to use) to put your specific intention or goal into it. Reiki programming is simple and powerful as the symbols such as **Cho Ku Rei or Dai ko Myo** are powerful symbols and they boost the crystal's energy & healing power for the highest possible good of the concerned person. This method can be used for any crystal. It enhances the crystal's natural vibrations and effectiveness.

2.  **Breath Work**: Hold the crystal in your hands and take deep breaths. As you exhale, focus on your goal. Visualize your breath carrying your intention into the crystal. See the crystal absorbing this energy. This simple method aligns the crystal with your desired outcome. It boosts the crystal's healing power.

3.  **Affirmations**: Hold the crystal and speak or think positive statements about your goal. Affirmations align the crystal with your goals. Say affirmations such as "I program this crystal for better health and

wellness. This crystal brings strength, healing and vitality to my body and mind." It is a simple way to boost the crystal's effectiveness and healing properties. Repeat this affirmation while focusing on your intention for improved health.

4. **Visualization**: Hold the crystal. Picture a bright light (White, Golden, Pink, Violet- depending on your goal ) around it. Imagine this light filling the crystal. Focus on your goal, like healing or love. See the light carrying your intention into the crystal. This simple method helps the crystal absorb and amplify your goal. Keep visualizing that your goal is accomplished and think how you would feel about it.

There may be several other methods to program the crystals, but I found the above ones simple to follow.

# Chapter 8

# Lifestyle Changes & Nutritional Support

During the healing journey, my daily routine started with 20-25 minutes of Yoga, followed by 15-20 minutes of combined practice of Reiki, chakra healing & mantra Jaap.

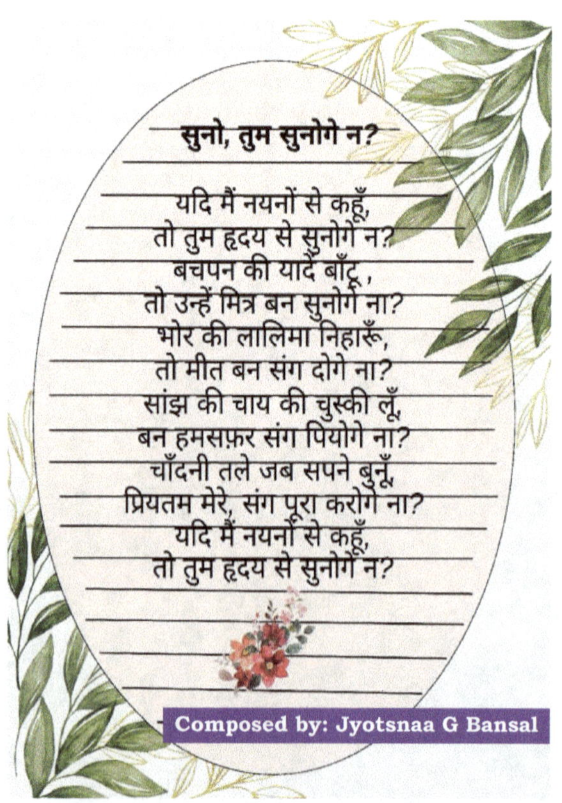


Evenings comprised of friendly evening walk with Navit, which was our time to interact about how was the day for both of us. That was the time when Navit would listen patiently to my all chit-chat (read – *silly talks*), so I could express my feelings, my thoughts, my opinions uninterruptedly and without any judgement. Infact, his humorous comments made me laugh most of the times, helping me to let go of my tensions, anxiety & stress.

Now, while practicing the healing holistic modalities, there was need of nutritional support and dietary adjustments. So, to start with, I first of all, stopped consuming all packaged fast food and cold-drinks and shifted to nutrient- rich foods and supplements.

In this process, I, by chance, consumed Black Pepper in all my food items. Later on, I discovered through one of the YouTube Videos, that ***Black Pepper is the Magical Herb*** for persons suffering from Thyroid issues.

However, I did not follow any particular Thyroid-Friendly Diet. I just followed my thoughts & gut instincts. There were times, when instead of consuming full diet, I had only Salad. This helped a lot as detoxification process.

# Chapter 9
# Holistic Harmony: Balancing Mind, Body and Spirit

Holistic Harmony: Balancing Mind, Body and Spirit is about understanding how our Mental, Physical and Spiritual health are all connected. This idea teaches us that taking care of each aspect is crucial for overall well-being. It is not just about treating illnesses, but also about living a balanced life that includes good mental health, physical health and a sense of spiritual fulfillment. This approach helps us feel better as a whole and can prevent health problems before they start. By learning how these parts of us work together, we can make better choices to keep ourselves healthy and can achieve greater harmony in our lives.

❖ **Balancing Physical, Emotional and Spiritual well-being**

It involves nurturing all aspects of ourselves to achieve a state of overall health. Physically, this means taking care of the body through proper nutrition, exercise and rest.

Emotionally, it involves managing stress, expressing feelings in healthy ways and fostering positive & healthy relationships.

Spiritually, it encompasses finding deeper meaning and connection in life, which might include meditation, prayer, listening to music or nature walks. When these elements are in harmony, individuals often experience increased vitality, improved mental clarity and a greater sense of peace, contributing to a more fulfilled, harmonious and balanced life.

## ❖ Importance of Self-Awareness & Self-care

Self-awareness is key to good health and happiness. It means knowing your body, feelings, thoughts, needs and actions well. It helps you understand what makes you healthy or unwell.

By being self-aware, you can notice when you are stressed, tired, or need a break, also you can spot signs of stress or illness early. This knowledge lets you make better choices about eating, resting and exercising. It also helps you handle stress and emotions better, leading to a calmer and happier life. Overall, Self-awareness is key to taking care of your body and mind, helping you stay healthy and improve your well-being.

Simply put, knowing yourself well is crucial for a healthier, happier life.

## ❖ Importance of Mindfulness for Stress Management

Mindfulness means paying full attention to what is happening right now. It involves focusing on the present moment calmly. Practicing mindfulness can reduce stress, improve your mood and help you feel more relaxed. It also helps you make better choices about your health, like eating right and getting enough sleep.

Mindfulness also improves concentration and makes you more aware of life's joys, enhancing overall happiness. Physically, it can lower blood pressure, reduce chronic pain and strengthen the immune system. This can lead to better mental health and a stronger immune system.

Regular mindfulness can lead to better sleep and more energy. Overall, mindfulness supports both mental and physical well-being, making you healthier and happier.

### ❖ Finding harmony in life's challenges

Finding harmony in life's challenges means seeking balance during tough times. It involves accepting that problems are part of life, facing them with a calm and open mind and learning from them instead of resisting. By doing this, you reduce stress and increase your ability to handle difficulties calmly. This approach promotes mental peace, which is crucial for good health. Harmony comes from managing your time well between work, relaxation and fun.

Ultimately, finding harmony helps you navigate life's ups and downs more smoothly and happily in a healthier, more positive way.

### ❖ Exploring Alternative Healing Therapies

After struggling with persistent health issues that conventional medicine could not fully address, I turned to alternative & holistic methods like Yoga, Reiki energy Healing and other holistic practices. These practices not only alleviated my symptoms but also enhanced my overall well-being.

Sharing this journey is important to me because it opens up a world of healing possibilities that many might not consider. By embracing these gentle yet powerful approaches, I found a path to better health that was both transformative and enlightening. It led me to discover the profound benefits of alternative healing practices and new ways to manage my health challenges effectively and naturally.

### ❖ Healing Affirmations

Healing affirmations are positive statements repeated often to promote mental and physical health and over-all well-being. They help replace negative thoughts with hopeful beliefs. By saying these affirmations, you focus your mind on healing and positivity. This can boost your mood, reduce stress, supporting your body's natural ability to heal and maintain health.

Some examples of Affirmations for thyroid health and vitality:

- My thyroid is healthy and functioning perfectly.

- My energy levels are stable and abundant.

- I am full of vitality and my thyroid is strong.

- My thyroid health is improving every day.

- My body is in complete harmony and balance.

- I am healing and my thyroid is balancing.

## ❖ Visualizations

Visualization techniques mean using your imagination to see positive images or situations in your mind. By imagining yourself achieving goals or being in peaceful settings, you can boost your mood and motivation. The practice is based on the idea that your mind and body are interconnected and that your thoughts can influence your physical state. By thinking about good things happening or relaxing scenes, you can help reduce stress, improve your focus and feel better overall. Regular visualization can improve focus, reduce stress and enhance overall well-being, making it a powerful tool for both mental and physical health.

## ❖ Guided Meditations

Guided meditation is a practice for relaxation and stress reduction that involves meditation led by another person or mentor ( in person, audio or video) who provides explicit instructions throughout the session. It can be very effective, especially for beginners in meditation or those who prefer structured meditation sessions.

Guided meditation can prove beneficial for overall health, including reduced stress, lower blood pressure, reduced anxiety and depression symptoms, better sleep and improved immune system function.

However, it should not replace professional treatment but can be used as a complementary practice.

## ❖ Building Support Networks, Seeking Professional Guidance

Building a support network can prove beneficial and can be helpful in managing your thyroid condition better. Start by joining thyroid health groups online where you can meet others facing similar challenges. Talk openly with friends and family about your thyroid condition; they can offer emotional support and understanding. Connect with a healthcare professional who specializes in thyroid health for professional guidance. Share experiences and tips with others in support forums. Together, you can exchange useful advice, encouragement and keep each other motivated on your health journeys. This network becomes a valuable resource for coping and healing.

Engaging with like-minded individuals helps you feel less isolated, gain new knowledge and receive emotional support. This makes dealing with thyroid issues easier.

Ach. Bhavna Bhatia

Prof. Ashok Bhatia

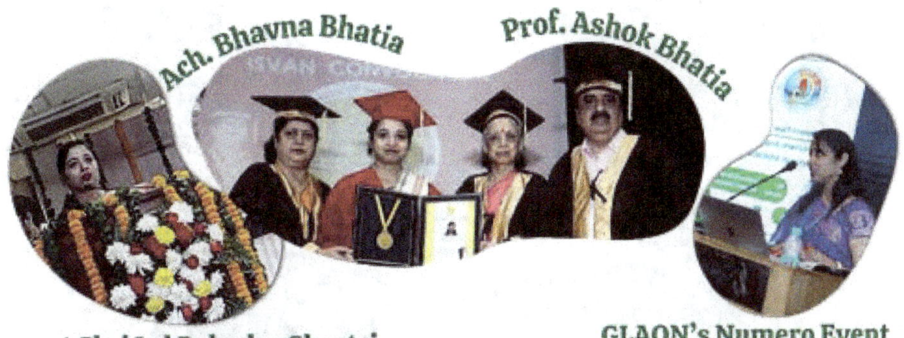

at Shri Lal Bahadur Shastri National Sanskrit University

GLAON's Numero Event at Radisson Blu, Dwarka

**Presented Research Papers on Different Topics**

Mr. Ankit Batra

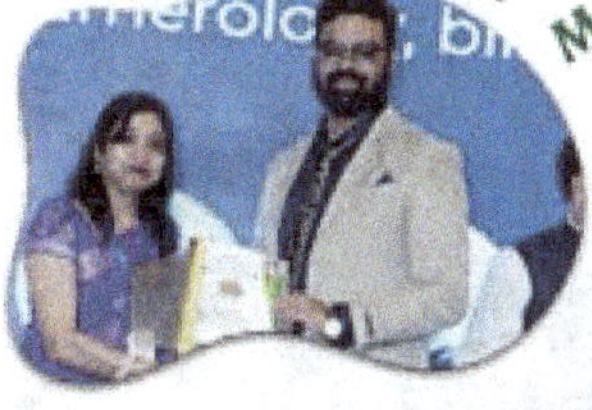

Mr. Sidhharrth S Kumaar

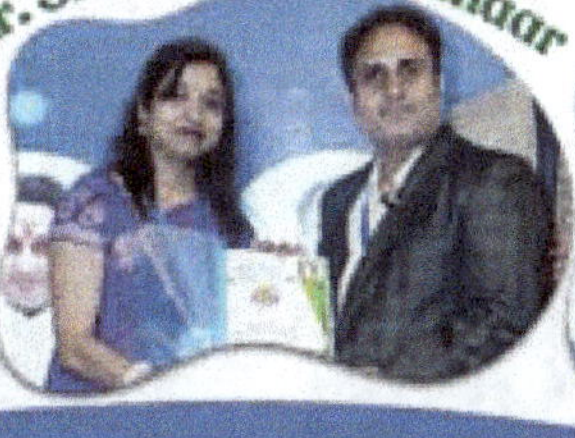

Mr. Kapil Sailley

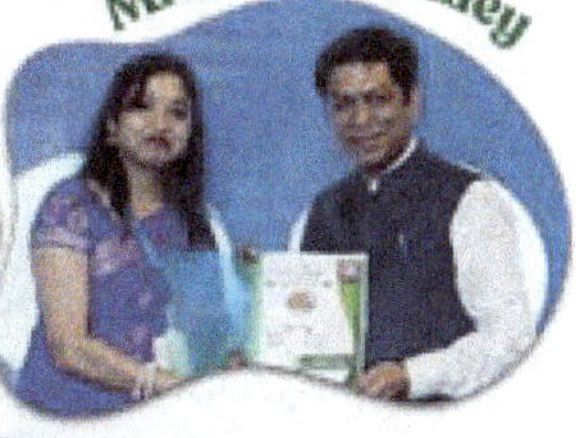

Mr. Sumeet Kr Tyagi

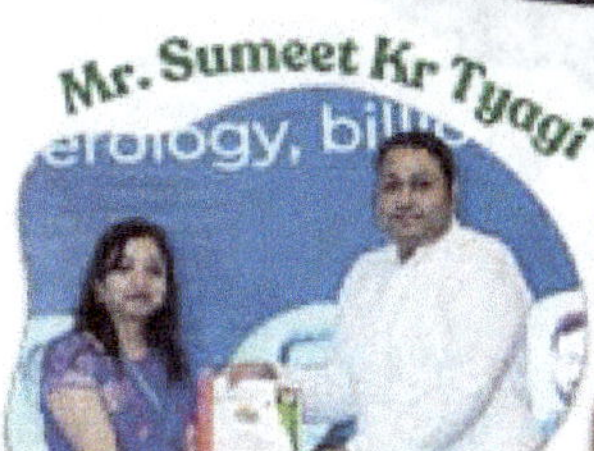

Mr. Arvind Rathan

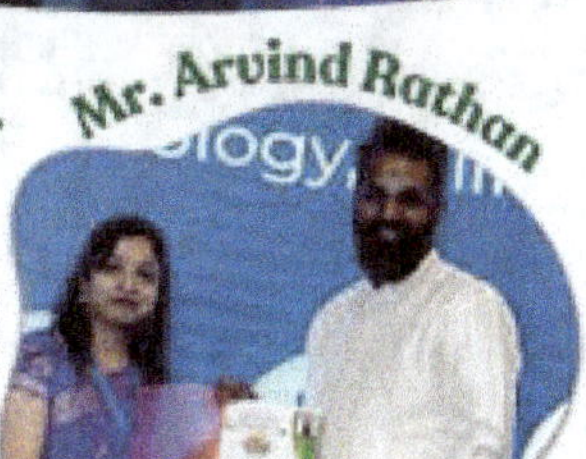

Mr. Gautham Azad

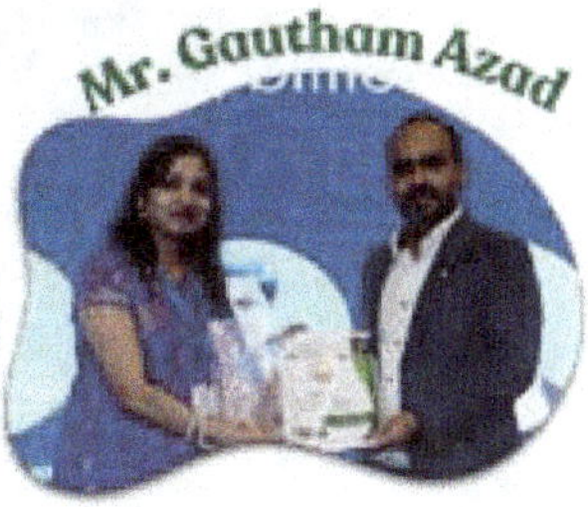

**Presented Numero Research Paper to Eminent Numerologists**

Performed at the First Offline Event (April 2023)
of Global Alliance of Numerologists,
Radisson Blu, Dwarka, New Delhi

Given presentations & provided counseling support to students in various schools as *Volunteer for Project by Department of School Education & Literacy (DoSEL), Ministry of Education, Government of India.*

at Nakshatra 2023,
Pragati Maidan, New Delhi
Smt. Krishna Teerath
Ach. Bhavna Bhatia
with
Prof. Ashok Bhatia
DEEP SECRETS of NAME
with
Prof. Milind Sudhakar Marathe
Chairman - National Book Trust, India
(Organizer of World Book Fair)
with Mr. J. C. Chaudhry
Founder & Chairman Emeritus at
Aakash Educational Services Ltd (AESL)
CAREERWILL APP
o Learn ...
DEEP SECRETS of NAME
Maths Wizard
Rakesh Yadav
Founder
Careerwill App
with
Sandeep Sharma
Maths Educator
Ex-Inspector (BSF)

# Hypothyroidism Healed

## Combined Holistic Approach: Yoga, Reiki, Mantra & Crystals

**"Hypothyroidism Healed"** is Jyotsnaa's own battle with hypothyroidism where alternative and holistic healing methods meet personal triumph. Through the pages of this book, readers will discover: a roadmap to wellness through spiritual wisdom & holistic approaches to thyroid health that is actionable, accessible, transformative and inspiring.

Faced with the challenges of stress, fatigue, anxiety, weight gain and emotional turmoil, Jyotsnaa was diagnosed with thyroid issues after her father's untimely demise.

Initially for 2 months, traditional medicines & treatment were undertaken to control the situation. But Jyotsnaa & her husband, **Adv. Navit Bansal**, both were not comfortable with the idea of life-long medication. Which paved the path for the journey of exploring the transformative power of alternative medicine & healing modalities.

With certain **Yoga poses** tailored for thyroid health, the subtle energy of **Self-Healing Reiki sessions**, the **therapeutic properties of crystals** and the transformative power of **mantras & meditation** alongwith a shift to homeopathic medicines, lifestyle & dietary changes Jyotsnaa started her healing journey, managing symptoms and nurturing inner harmony.

Her husband, Navit, stood by her throughout the challenging journey whether it was following daily rituals religiously or lifestyle & dietary changes. His unwavering support & care was instrumental in quitting the traditional methods, which could have resulted in life-long medication.

This book lists most of the practices Jyotsnaa followed in consultation with experts in the relevant fields:

1. Thyroid based Yoga poses, with pics & benefits, which includes yoga poses to improve metabolism, to reduce stress & anxiety.

2. Reiki & Chakra Healing.

3. Certain Chakra mantras & other Jaap mantras

4. Thyroid specific crystals

❖ Also, a Mnemonic is also shared, conceptualized by herself, **to learn 12 Zodiacs in a sequence in an easy way.** This might be helpful for the beginners in Astrology & Numerology.

Explore the inspiring real-life healing journey of Jyotsnaa. After the loss of her father, she faced a diagnosis of thyroid issues. With the unwavering support of her husband, **Adv. Navit Bansal**, they decided not to rely on lifelong medication. Through expert & careful guidance, Jyotsnaa embraced the transformative power of various alternative and holistic healing methods, emerging victorious. Today, she leads a healthy life without any thyroid medication, Thanks to practices like **Yoga, Reiki, Crystals, Mantras and Meditation** which helped her in restoring **balance to Mind, Body and Spirit**.

Whether you are facing thyroid challenges or simply seeking a path to greater well-being, this book provides you empowering insights to embark on a journey of self-discovery, resilience and profound healing from within.

# Learn 12 Zodiacs in a minute
by *Jyotsnaa G Bansal*

|  |  | |  |
|---|--------|---|----------|
| 1. | **A**ries | **A** | **A**gain |
| 2. | **T**aurus | **T** | **T**he |
| 3. | **G**emini | **G** | **G**alaxy |
| 4. | **C**ancer | **C** | **C**herished |
| 5. | **L**eo | **L** | **L**egendary |
| 6. | **V**irgo | **V** | **V**ictory |
| 7. | **L**ibra | **L** | **L**auded by |
| 8. | **S**corpio | **S** | **S**tars, |
| 9. | **S**agittarius | **S** | **S**igns, |
| 10. | **C**apricorn | **C** | **C**onstellations |
| 11. | **A**quarius | **A** | **A**nd |
| 12. | **P**isces | **P** | **P**lanets |

# Resources

1. Shiv Puran by Gita Press, Gorakhpur

2. Crystal Prescriptions by Judy Hall

3. The Crystal Bible by Judy Hall

4. The Magic of Crystals in Your Reiki Journey by Rinku Patel

5. Crystal Recipes by Rinku Patel

6. Art of Living - www.artofliving.org

7. American Thyroid Association – www.thyroid.org

8. Yogasanas by Yogaguru Swami Ramdev

9. Better All – www.betterall.net

10. Reiki Healing Foundation

11. The International Center for Reiki Training